Get **A**rt Smart

What Is Texture?

by Stephanie Fitzgerald

Crabtree Publishing Company

www.crabtreebooks.com

Crabtree Publishing Company

Author: Stephanie Fitzgerald
Publishing plan research and development:
 Sean Charlebois, Reagan Miller
 Crabtree Publishing Company
Editors: Reagan Miller
Proofreader: Kathy Middleton, Molly Aloian
Editorial director: Kathy Middleton
Photo research: Edward A. Thomas
Designer: Tammy West, Westgraphix LLC
Production coordinator: Margaret Amy Salter
Prepress technician: Margaret Amy Salter
Consultant: Julie Collins-Dutkiewicz, B.A., specialist in early
 childhood education, Sandy Waite, M.Ed., U.S. National
 Board Certified Teacher, author, and literacy consultant
Reading Consultant: Susan Nations, M.Ed.,
Author/Literacy Coach/Consultant in Literacy Development

Photographs and reproductions
Cover: © Lisa Maisonneuve; 1: Shutterock; 5, 23: iStockphoto; 7:
Terra Foundation for American Art, Chicago/Art Resource, NY; 9:
Museum of Modern Art, New York/The Bridgeman Art Library;
11: Louvre, Paris/The Bridgeman Art Library; 13: Oratorio di
Galla Placidia, Ravenna, Italy/The Bridgeman Art Library; 15:
Germanisches Nationalmuseum, Nuremberg, Germany/The
Bridgeman Art Library; 17, 19: © Edward A. Thomas; 21:
Louvre, Paris/Peter Willi/The Bridgeman Art Library.

Front cover (main image): A young artist is excited at all of the texture possibilities.
Title page: A young boy cuddles a soft toy.
Written, developed, and produced by RJF Publishing LLC

Library and Archives Canada Cataloguing in Publication

Fitzgerald, Stephanie
 What is texture? / Stephanie Fitzgerald.

(Get art smart)
Includes index.
ISBN 978-0-7787-5127-4 (bound).--ISBN 978-0-7787-5141-0 (pbk.)

 1. Texture (Art)--Juvenile literature. I. Title. II. Series: Get art smart

N7430.5.F58 2009   j701'.8   C2009-903592-8

Library of Congress Cataloging-in-Publication Data

Fitzgerald, Stephanie.
 What is texture? / Stephanie Fitzgerald.
  p. cm. -- (Get art smart)
 Includes index.
 ISBN 978-0-7787-5141-0 (pbk. : alk. paper) -- ISBN 978-0-7787-5127-4 (re-
inforced library binding : alk. paper)
 1. Texture (Art)--Juvenile literature. I. Title. II. Series.

N7430.5.F55 2009
701'.8--dc22
                                                     2009022917

Crabtree Publishing Company

www.crabtreebooks.com   1-800-387-7650

**Published
in Canada
Crabtree Publishing**
616 Welland Ave.
St. Catharines, Ontario
L2M 5V6

**Published in
the United States
Crabtree Publishing**
PMB16A
350 Fifth Ave., Suite 3308
New York, NY 10118

**Published in the
United Kingdom
Crabtree Publishing**
Maritime House
Basin Road North, Hove
BN41 1WR

**Published
in Australia
Crabtree Publishing**
386 Mt. Alexander Rd.
Ascot Vale (Melbourne)
VIC 3032

Contents

Kinds of Texture

Texture is the way something looks and feels. We can feel texture when we touch something. We can also see the texture of something with our eyes. **Rough**, **smooth**, **bumpy**, and **soft** are all types of textures. A cotton ball has a soft texture. Sand has a rough texture.

Sand feels rough when you touch it.

Artists Use Texture

We can add textures to artworks in many ways. When we paint, we can use watercolor paints on shiny paper. The picture we make will look flat and smooth.

Franklin Park, Boston, by Maurice Prendergast (1890s)

The artist used watercolor paints to make this picture. It looks flat and smooth.

Making Thick Layers

We can add thick layers of paint to a painting. We can put a lot of paint on the brush and make short lines. This can give the painting a bumpy texture. We can also use a sponge to paint. Painting with a sponge gives the picture a rough texture.

The Starry Night, by Vincent van Gogh (1889)

The artist used thick layers of paint to give this picture a bumpy texture.

What We Paint On

Sometimes artists paint pictures on **canvas**. Canvas is a kind of cloth. It can give the picture a rough texture. A long time ago, people painted pictures on paper made from plants. The paper gave the painting a rough texture.

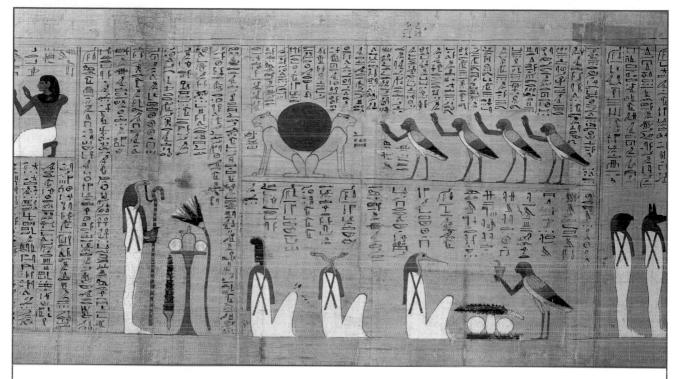

Papyrus painting from ancient Egypt (about 1000 B.C.)

This painting was done on paper made from plants.

Texture from Tiles

We can use tiny tiles to make art. We can create a picture by placing different colored tiles in a **pattern**. Each tile is smooth, but together the tiles create a bumpy picture.

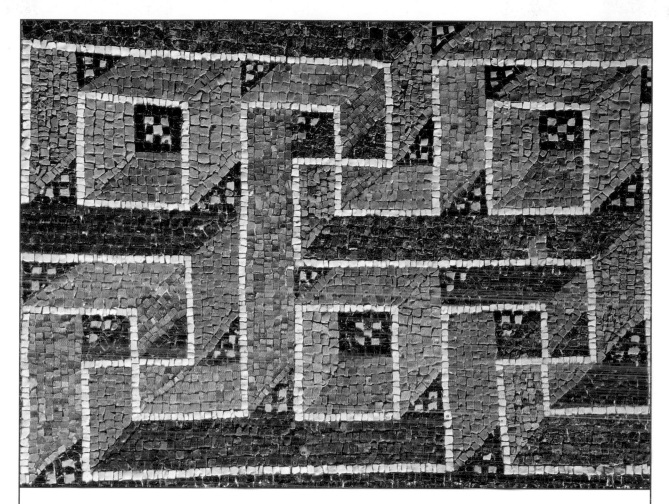

Byzantine mosaic (400s A.D.)

This pattern was made with many small tiles.

Texture in Clay

There are many other ways we can add texture to artwork. To add texture to art made of clay, we can carve lines and shapes into the clay.

Tile from Konstanz, Germany (made about 1300)

The artist carved the shape of an eagle in this clay tile.

Gluing on Texture

We can also glue objects to a picture to add texture. Yarn, cotton balls, dried pasta, and colored sand all add texture.

Have you ever glued pasta onto one of your pictures?

Making a Rubbing

We can make a smooth piece of art look as if it has texture. We can do this by coloring over a rough material, such as a leaf or a coin. This is called making a **rubbing**. To make a rubbing, lay your paper over the rough material and rub a crayon over the page.

This girl is making a rubbing of a leaf.

Texture in Drawings

We can add texture to our drawings, too. We can use different kinds of lines, shapes, and colors to give our drawings texture. We can show the soft texture of a lion's mane by drawing thin, curving lines close to each other.

Lion Resting, by Rembrandt van Rijn (1600s)

The artist used many thin lines to make this lion's mane look soft.

Texture in Nature

Many artists get ideas from things they see in nature. The next time you are outside, look at all the different textures you see. There is art all around you!

What textures can you find in nature?

Words to Know

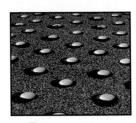
bumpy

canvas

pattern

rough

smooth

soft

Find Out More

Books

The Art Book for Children: Book Two. New York: Phaidon Press, 2007.

Dickins, Rosie. *The Children's Book of Art.* New York: Scholastic Inc., 2005.

Web sites

A Lifetime of Color
www.alifetimeofcolor.com

Fun craft ideas from Crayola
www.crayola.com

Printed in the USA—CG